Adult Coloring Books

ABSTRACT DESIGNS

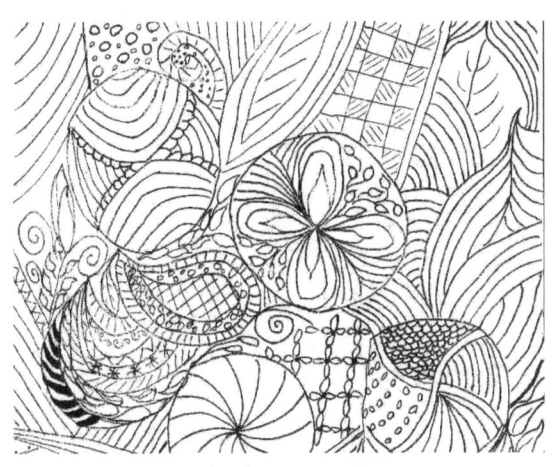

By: Asha Simpson

ISBN-13 978-1516868117

Asha Simpson

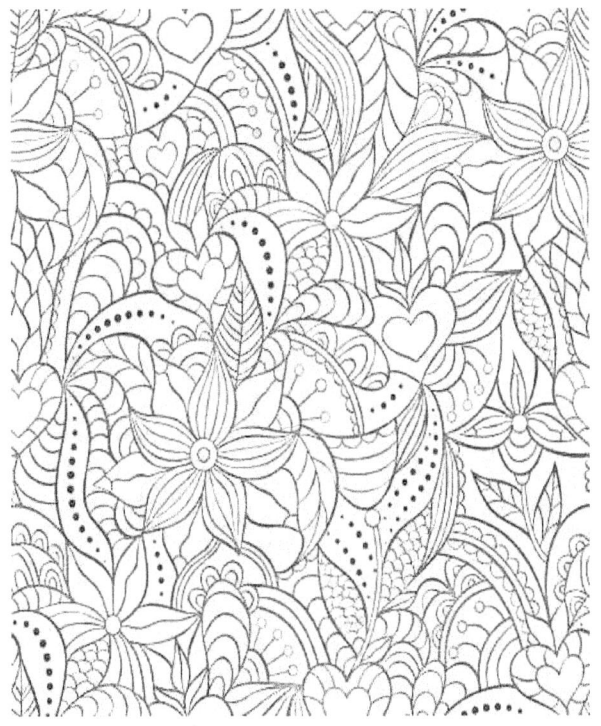

COLORS

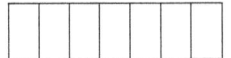

COLORS

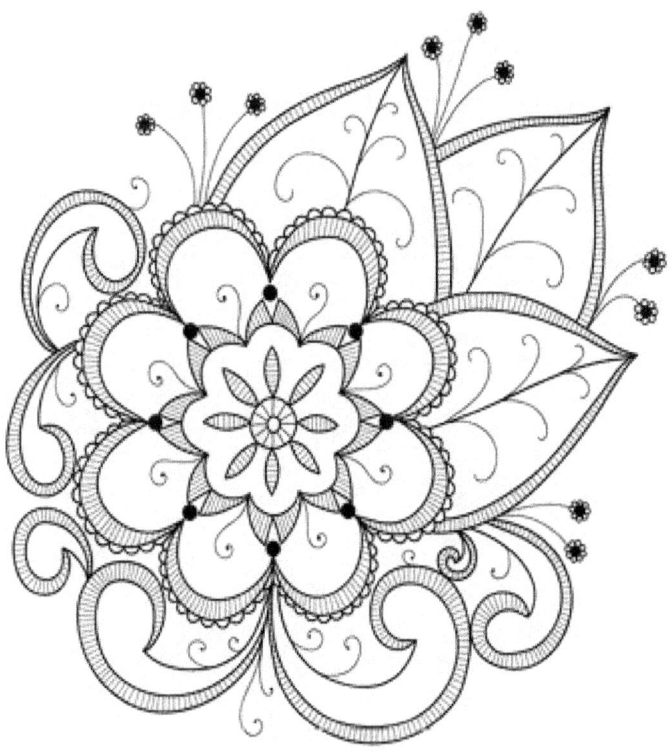

COLORS

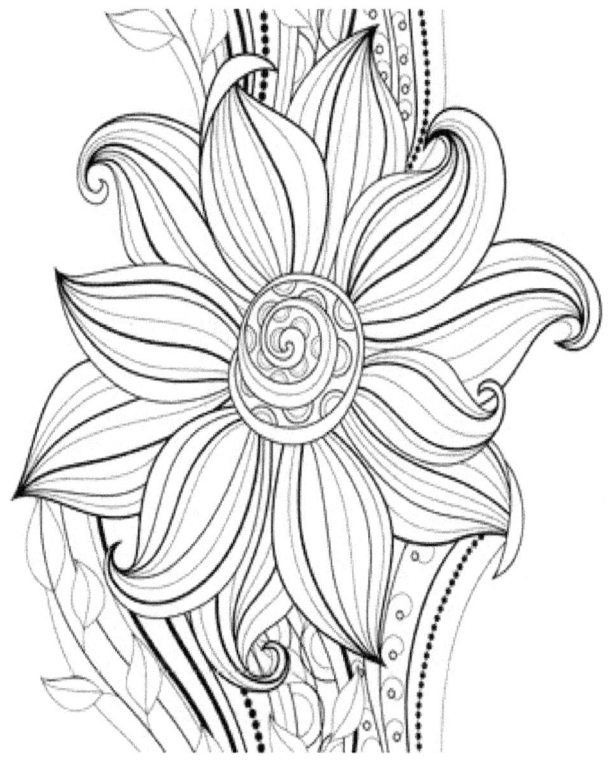

COLORS

Asha Simpson

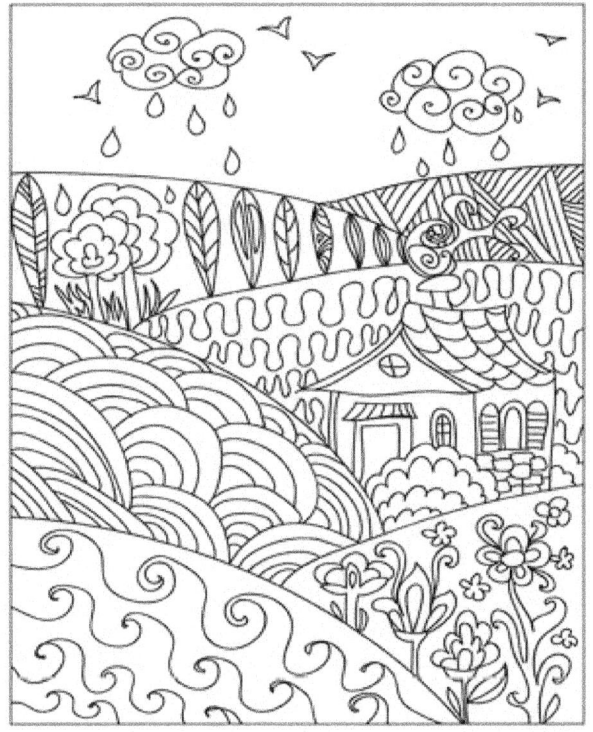

COLORS

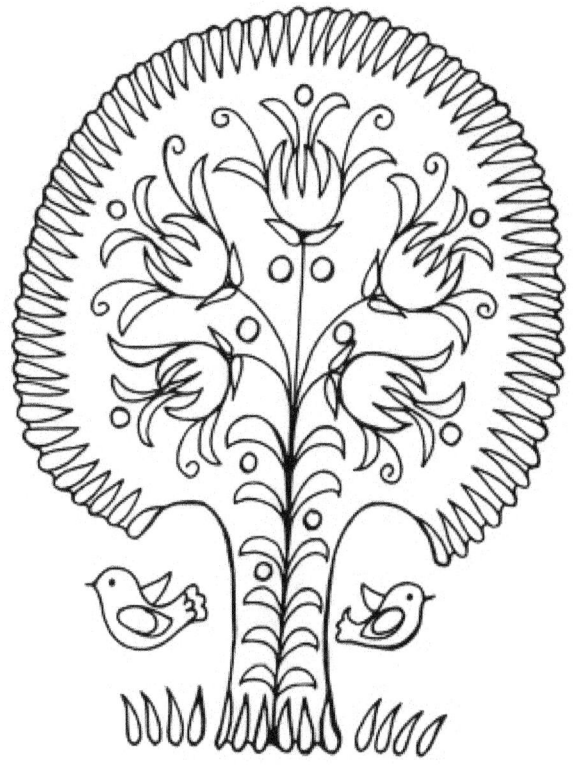

COLORS

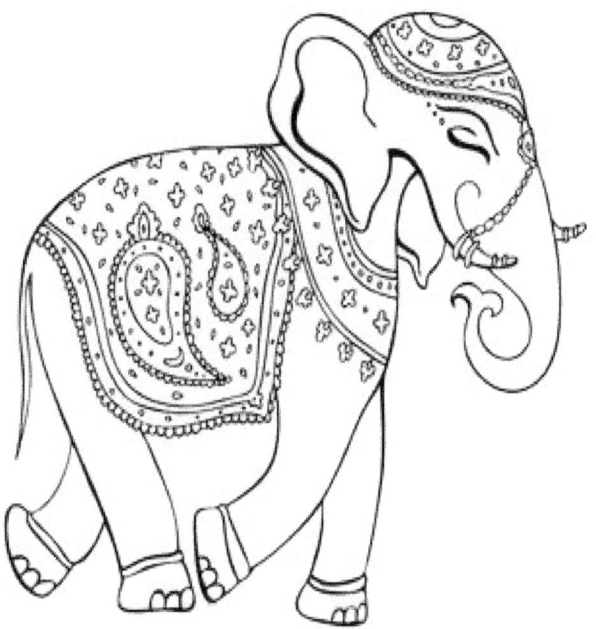

COLORS

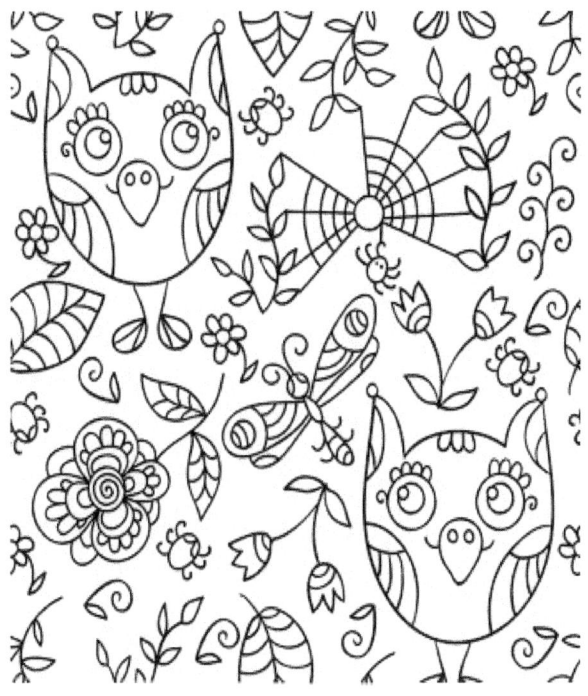

COLORS

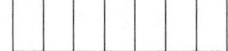

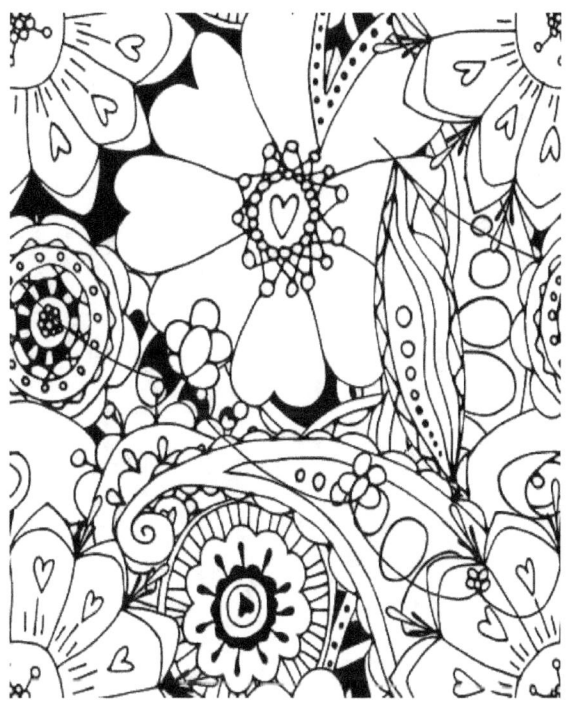

COLORS

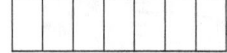

COLORS

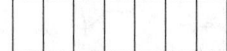

Asha Simpson

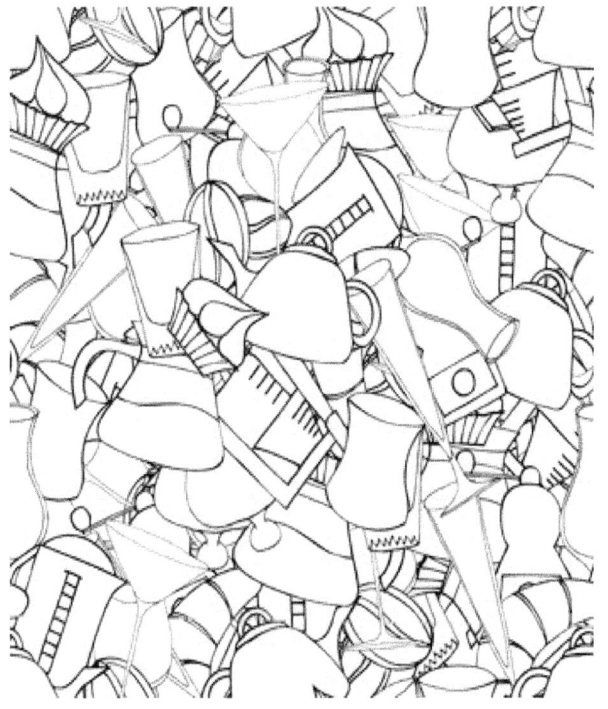

COLORS

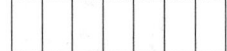

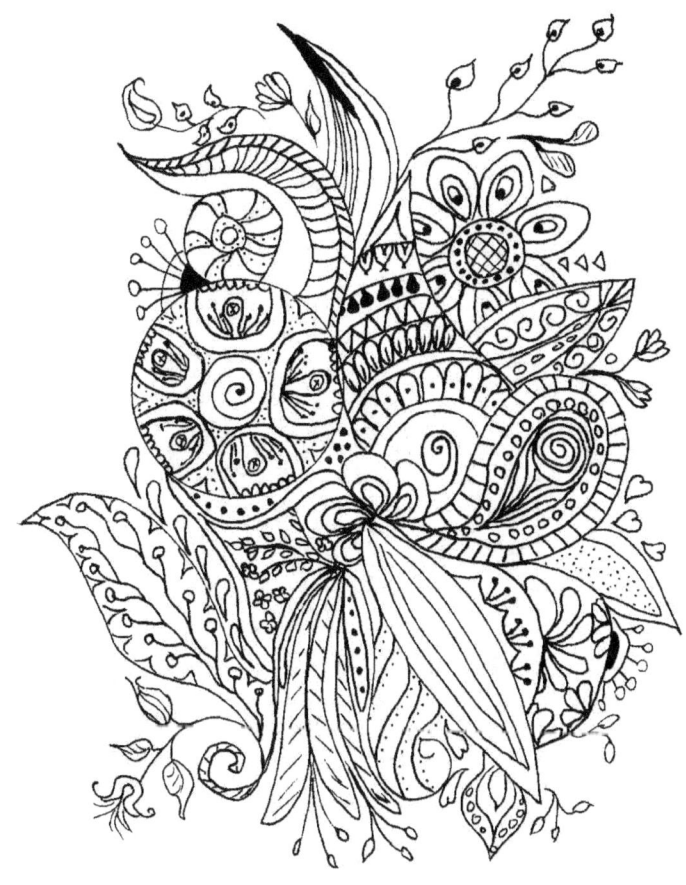

COLORS

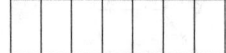

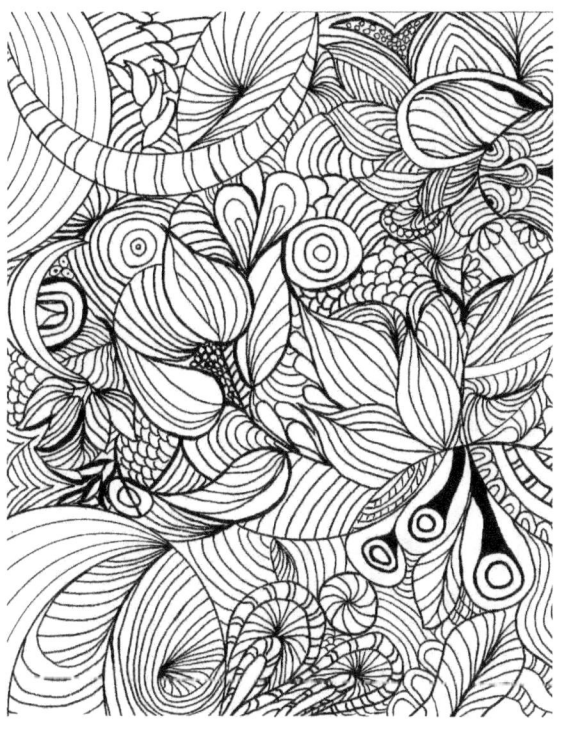

COLORS

COLORS

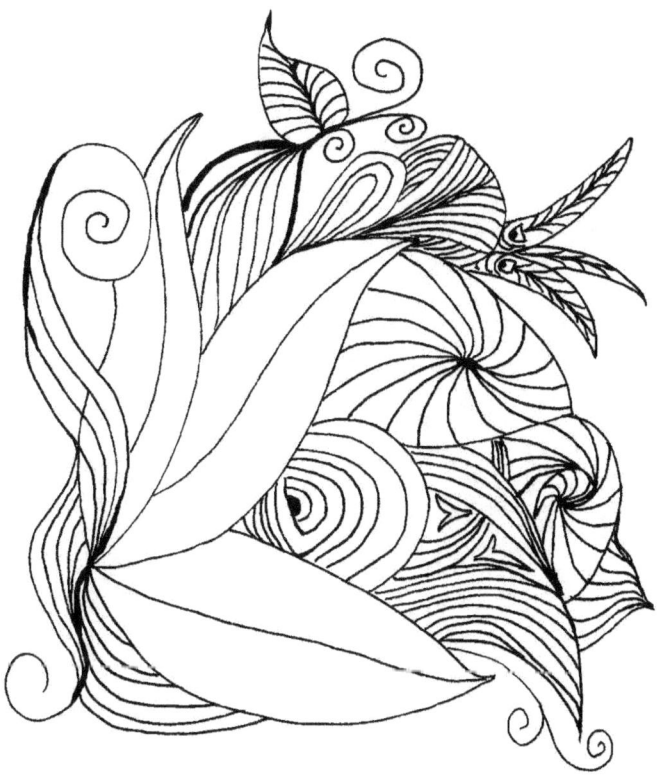

COLORS

Asha Simpson

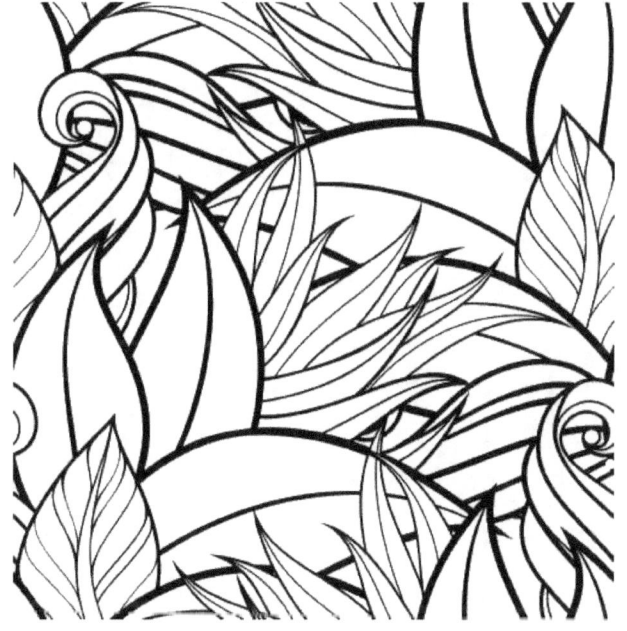

COLORS

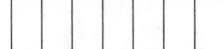

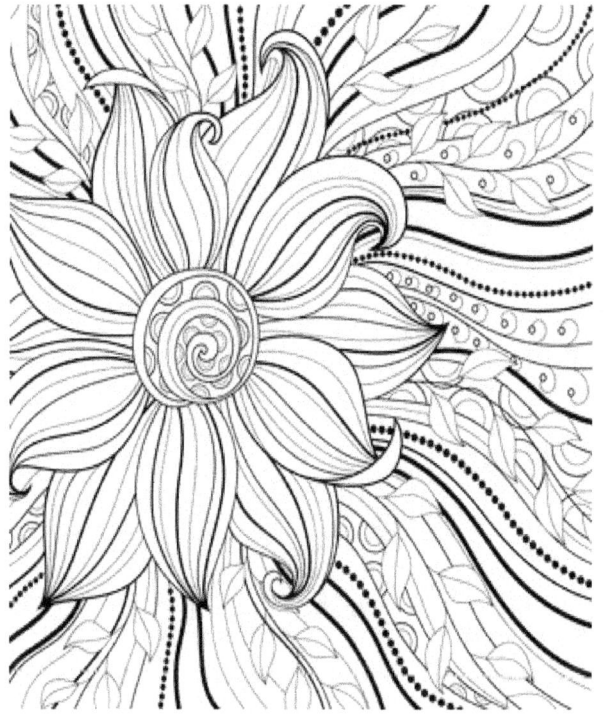

COLORS

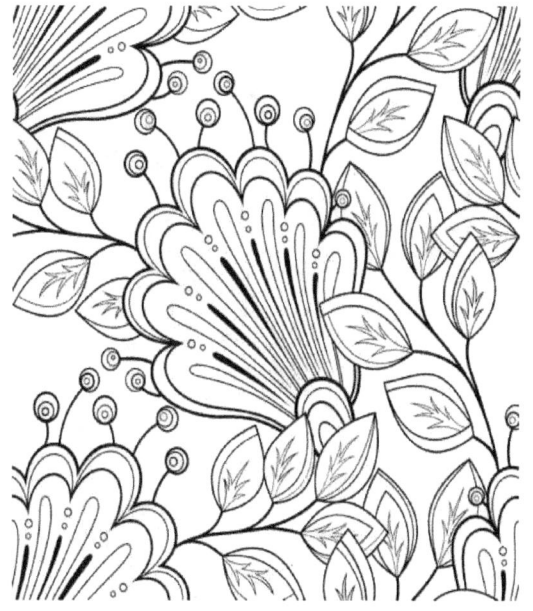

COLORS

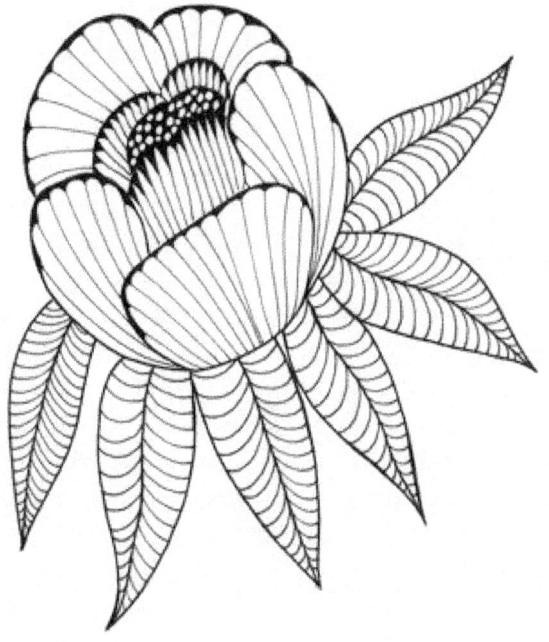

COLORS

Asha Simpson

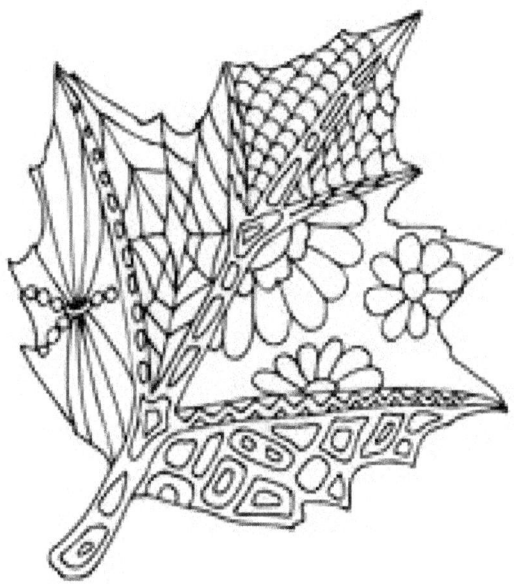

COLORS

Asha Simpson

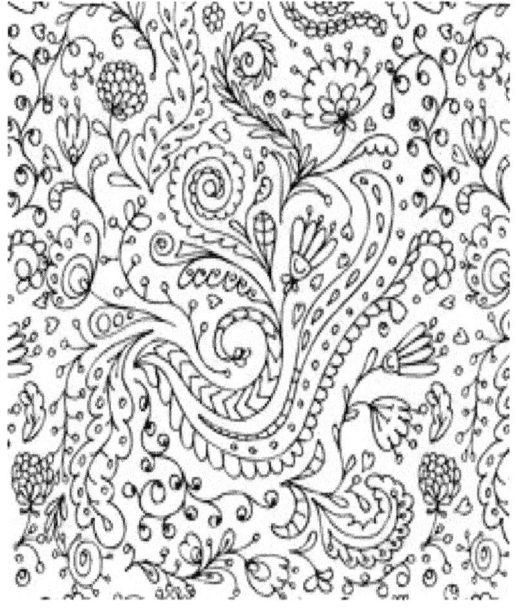

COLORS

Asha Simpson

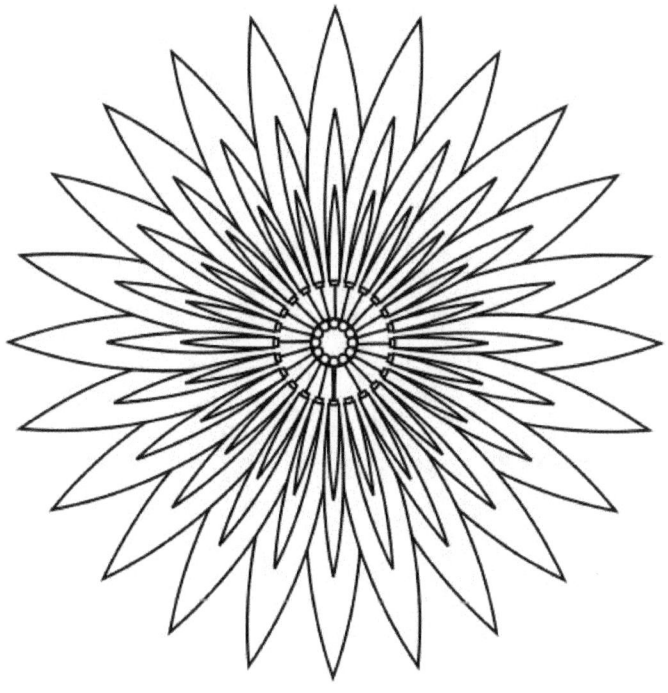

COLORS

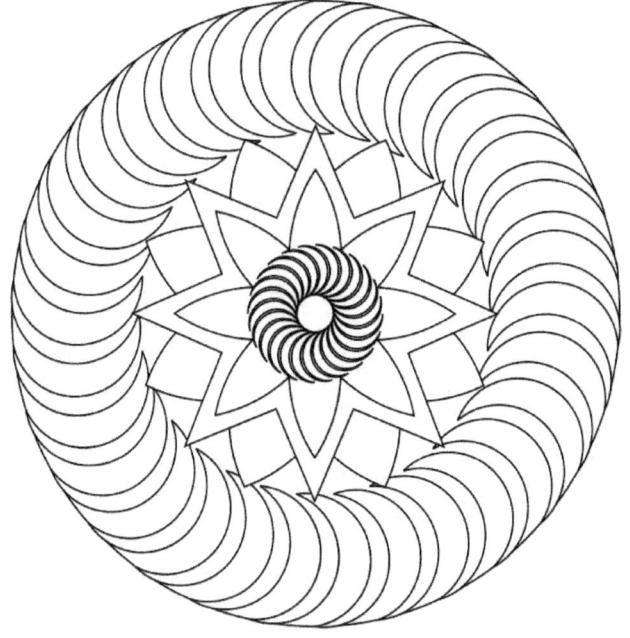

COLORS

COLORS

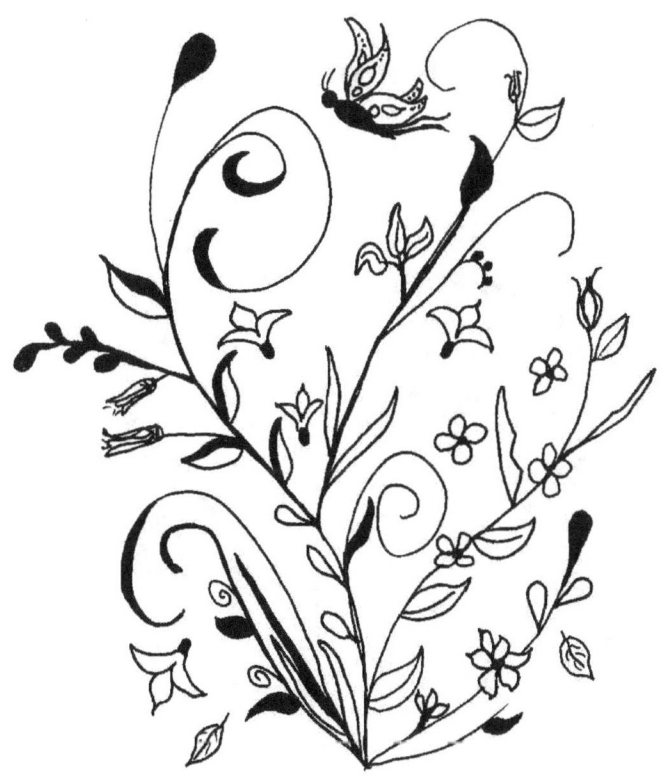

Other Coloring Books from

InfoEbooksOnline

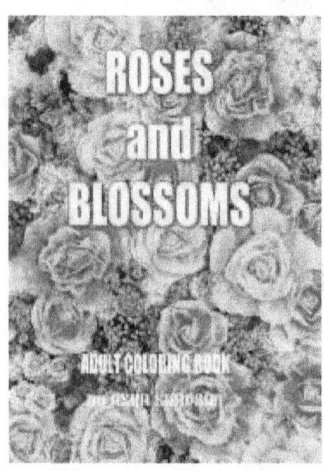

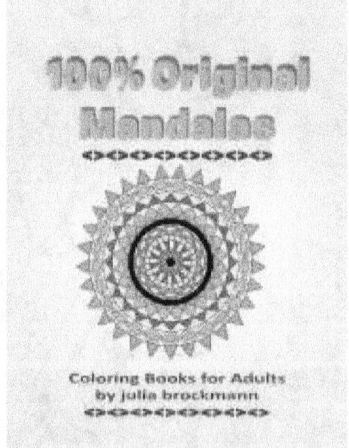

INFOEBOOKSONLINE

InfoEbooksOnline s a well known publishing company which specializes in lifestyle books of many kinds for both adult and children.

Their philosophy is:

Work hard and enjoy life through activities that replenish the body and the soul.

Paperback products can be sourced through

CreateSpace.com

InfoEbooksOnline.com

WordSearchandPuzzles.com